MAHAKALA

and Other Insect-Eating Dinosaurs

by **Dougal Dixon**

illustrated by **Steve Weston and James Field**

PICTURE WINDOW BOOKS
Minneapolis, Minnesota

Picture Window Books
151 Good Counsel Drive
P.O. Box 669
Mankato, MN 56002-0669
877-845-8392
www.picturewindowbooks.com

Printed in the United States of America.

 All books published by Picture Window Books
are manufactured with paper containing at
least 10 percent post-consumer waste.

Library of Congress Cataloging-in-Publication Data
Dixon, Dougal.
Mahakala and other insect-eating dinosaurs /
by Dougal Dixon ; illustrated by Steve Weston and
James Field.
p. cm. — (Dinosaur Find)
Includes index.
ISBN 978-1-4048-5177-1 (library binding)
1. Dinosaurs—Juvenile literature. 2. Dinosaurs—
Food—Juvenile literature. I. Weston, Steve, ill. II. Field,
James, 1959- ill. III. Title.
QE861.5.D598 2009
567.912—dc22   2008043383

Acknowledgments
This book was produced for Picture Window Books
by Bender Richardson White, U.K.

Illustrations by James Field (pages 4–5, 9, 15, 17, 21)
and Steve Weston (cover and pages 7, 11, 13, 19).
Diagrams by Stefan Chabluk.

Photographs: Frank Lane Picture Agency pages 6
(Wendy Dennis/FLPA), 12 (Wendy Dennis/FLPA),
18 (Panda Photo/FLPA), iStockphoto pages 8 (phil
morley), 10 (Andrew Howe), 14 (Yuriy Soshnikov),
16 (Cornelia Pithart), 20 (Chris Fourie)

Consultant: John Stidworthy, Scientific Fellow of
the Zoological Society, London, and former
Lecturer in the Education Department, Natural
History Museum, London.

Types of dinosaurs
In the Dinosaur Find books,
a red shape at the top of a
left-hand page shows the
animal was a meat-eater.
A green shape shows it was
a plant-eater.

**Just how big—or small—
were they?**
Dinosaurs were many different
sizes. We have compared their
size to one of the following:

Chicken
2 feet (60 centimeters) tall
Weight 6 pounds (2.7 kilograms)

Adult person
6 feet (1.8 meters) tall
Weight 170 pounds (76.5 kg)

Elephant
10 feet (3 m) tall
Weight 12,000 pounds
(5,400 kg)

TABLE OF CONTENTS

WHAT'S INSIDE?

Dinosaurs! These dinosaurs survived by eating insects and other small animals that lived between 230 million and 65 million years ago. Find out how these dinosaurs lived and what they have in common with today's animals.

3

LIFE AS AN INSECT-EATER

Dinosaurs lived between 230 million and 65 million years ago. The world did not look the same then. Much of the land and many of the seas were not in the same places as today. But like today, insects lived everywhere and were eaten by all sorts of animals, including dinosaurs.

Dinosaurs of the deep, dark forest included medium-sized *Neimongosaurus* and little *Protarchaeopteryx* and *Sinosauropteryx*. All of these dinosaurs ate insects.

PATAGONYKUS

Pronunciation:
PAT-a-GON-ee-kus

Patagonykus was a swift little dinosaur that hunted small animals. Insects, spiders, and scorpions were part of its diet. With little arms and a single big claw on each hand, *Patagonykus* could scrape at the soil looking for food.

Risky hunters today

A modern meerkat hunts dangerous scorpions, just as *Patagonykus* did long ago.

Size Comparison

Patagonykus first bit off a scorpion's stinger before it could fight against the animal's snapping claws.

Neimongosaurus had a little head but gigantic hands. The dinosaur used the big claws on its hands to tear into the nests of termites and ants. *Neimongosaurus* feasted on the thousands of insects living there.

Ant-eaters today

Modern ant-eating animals, such as the Australian echidna, have big claws on their hands. They use these to rip their way into insect nests, just as *Neimongosaurus* once did.

Size Comparison

Once the inside of a termite nest was torn open, *Neimongosaurus* lapped up the tiny insects with its long tongue.

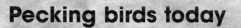

MAHAKALA

Pronunciation:
MA-ha-KAY-la

Mahakala looked just like a big bird as it darted through the woods. This dinosaur ate small creatures that it hunted on the ground. Insects must have made up most of its diet.

Pecking birds today

The modern starling finds its food on the ground, just as *Mahakala* did long ago.

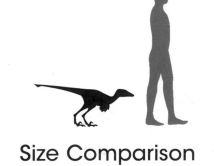

Size Comparison

Holding its head close
to the ground, *Mahakala*
could see and feed on
little insects that lived in
the soil.

TSAAGAN

Pronunciation:
SAA-gan

Tsaagan was one of the dinosaurs we call raptors. It was a clever hunter and could hunt both big and small prey. *Tsaagan* was a very active animal and needed lots of food to keep it going.

Insect-eaters today

Modern chimpanzees know where insects live. They can lift fallen trees and tear bark off of tree trunks to find them.

Size Comparison

Tsaagan knew where to find food. If it lifted a fallen tree, insects and other small creatures were often beneath it.

SINOSAUROPTERYX

Pronunciation:
SIGH-no-saw-OP-ter-icks

In dinosaur times, the forests and the forest floors were full of all kinds of insects. The smallest of the dinosaurs, such as *Sinosauropteryx*, were barely bigger than the largest insects that were around.

Big insects today

A modern dragonfly can grow very large. *Sinosauropteryx* would have once enjoyed finding such an insect for food.

Size Comparison

Sinosauropteryx had a problem when hunting a big beetle. The small dinosaur had to bite through the beetle's armor to get at the flesh.

PROTARCHAEOPTERYX

Pronunciation:
pro-TAR-kay-OP-ter-icks

Protarchaeopteryx had feathers on its body and tail. It pecked its way through the ground plants growing along the shores of lakes in the area that is now China. *Protarchaeopteryx* ate anything it came across—including insects.

Ground-pecking animals today

Flocks of modern chickens pecking at the soil eat up all of the insects they find, just as *Protarchaeopteryx* once did.

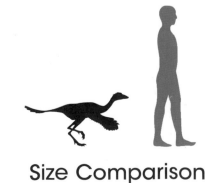

Size Comparison

When *Protarchaeopteryx* pecked away at the ground, no food was left behind.

SCIPIONYX

Pronunciation:
SKIP-ee-ON-icks

Unlike most dinosaurs of the time, *Scipionyx* was tiny. It hunted and ate insects. *Scipionyx* could have chased flying insects as they darted along the ground.

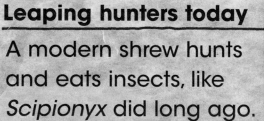

Leaping hunters today

A modern shrew hunts and eats insects, like *Scipionyx* did long ago.

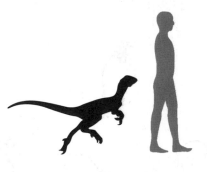

Size Comparison

When *Scipionyx* saw a big dragonfly buzzing past, it leapt after it.

STRUTHIOMIMUS

Pronunciation:
STROO-thee-o-MIM-mus

Struthiomimus lived in herds on open plains toward the end of the Age of Dinosaurs. It was bothered by swarms of flies and other insects. The insects gathered around to suck *Struthiomimus'* blood or lay eggs on its skin.

Insect fighters today

A modern ostrich bathes itself in dust to chase away insects on its skin. *Struthiomimus* probably once did the same.

Size Comparison

When *Struthiomimus* was attacked by insects, it fought back by scratching.

WHERE DID THEY GO?

Dinosaurs are extinct, which means that none of them are alive today. Scientists study rocks and fossils to find clues about what happened to dinosaurs.

People have different explanations about what happened. Some people think a huge asteroid that hit Earth caused all sorts of climate changes, which caused the dinosaurs to die. Others think volcanic eruptions caused the climate change and that killed the dinosaurs. No one knows for sure what happened to all of the dinosaurs.

GLOSSARY

armor—protective covering of plates, horns, spikes, or clubs used for fighting

claws—tough, usually curved fingernails or toenails

insects—small, six-legged animals; they include ants, bees, beetles, and flies

prey—an animal that is hunted and eaten for food

raptor—an animal that hunts

soil—another word for dirt

termites—insects that eat wood

To Learn More

More Books to Read

Clark, Neil, and William Lindsay. *1001 Facts About Dinosaurs.* New York: Dorling Kindersley, 2002.

Dixon, Dougal. *Dougal Dixon's Amazing Dinosaurs.* Honesdale, Pa.: Boyds Mills Press, 2007.

Holtz, Thomas R., and Michael Brett-Surman. *Jurassic Park Institute Dinosaur Field Guide.* New York: Random House, 2001.

On the Web

FactHound offers a safe, fun way to find educator-approved Internet sites related to this book.

Here's what you do:
1. Visit *www.facthound.com*
2. Choose your grade level.
3. Begin your search.

This book's ID number is 9781404851771

Index

Look for other books in the Dinosaur Find series: